Cracks in the Concrete

Cracks in the Concrete

**A Collection of Poems
by
James Goldiner**

Cracks in the Concrete

Published by Lotus Press
213 Muench Street
Harrisburg, PA 17102
Tel: 717 773 4810
Email: childsr1@verizon.net

ISBN No 978-0-615-51414-7
0615514146

Edited, cover design and author's photograph by Stewart Rein

Printed in the United States

Contents

For
Joan

Acknowledgement

I wish to thank Anne and Bill Pyne for their support, encouragement and enthusiasm

James Goldiner

Even Old Men can be Lucky Coins

i get an urgent call from the superintendent
about 2 weeks late
paul whiteman is sick he says
he won't eat and he's going fast
i rush out and can hardly
find paul rolled up in the sheets
with no clothes and no flesh
6 feet tall and down to 100 pounds
looking like the ghost of the real whiteman

i call for an ambulance

in a week he's dead

the superintendent on the other hand
collects the old man's checks
for the next 8 months
quits his job
an opens a bodega

The Art of Social Work

every day in sun light
i go to see the dying
and the dead
and anyone else
who happens to be there
it's work it feeds me
and it feeds anyone else
who happens to be around

it's odd but the dying
move in perpendiculars
playing bubble machines and radio
moving incognito with fig leaves

the dead don't move

they come for help
moving faster than they walk
moving in perpendiculars
some coming out of soup kettles
dripping vegetables and dripping paste
some can't walk at all
but they all come
expecting me to make the cure
to pass out bread and fish
and do a dance on water
re-arrange their lives
and do away with what they've done
or what's been done to them

so i give them a little of this here
a little of that there
fling a little something in the right spot
                              or the wrong spot
i tell them not to worry
that the sky is still there
and the worms will be back in spring

sometimes it works

Even Royalty finds it Rough Going Sometimes

i don't know what help this will be now
but in matters of the heart
almost everything is important

it was 1969 on the 7th of may
when i interviewed the king of spain
tall slender and with that lovely golden tooth

it seems he was temporarily
down on his luck
out of funds
out of love
and looking for both

of course when dealing with royalty
one can never be too careful
what with all the pretenders everywhere
when i asked for his credentials
he simply tipped his beret
and sure enough
it said genuine basque
and that was good enough for me

me and the king talked awhile
then the psychiatrist spoke with him
but you know how they are
always doubting truth
you would have been proud of the king

the way he handled this doctor
this meddler in unfamiliar things
after half an hour
this doc gave up
partly out of fear
when the king threatened
to beat shit out of him

i was able to help the king though
with money for a week's food
and rent at the hotel seventeen

but when it comes to love
we're all on our own

oh incidentally
after the king
i interviewed a happy rockerfeller
she was very happy

I'm Walking the Dogs

i'm walking the dogs on west 54th street
towards eleventh avenue
the temperature is 35, 40 degrees
a slight wind feels like it's coming off the plains

passing the centro maria
a young woman is smoking a
cigarette in the shadows

as i pass we acknowledge each other

the dogs are reading the
foot high brick wall
surrounding a tree in front
of the centro maria …for signs

as she steps towards the door to go inside
a pigeon flies out of those shadows
low to the ground

the woman is startled, only
for a moment
the dogs don't mention it

she takes one last deep inhale
and disappears just like the bird

Driving North

two weeks ago
very early in the day
passing through the fields above Bennett's Pond
the deer have been here before me

a light snow fell through the night

it's all silence except for the sound
of the snow still falling
and the wings of hawks circling above

the vegetation at the edge of the fields
brown and tan is barely moving
the milkweed pods and lacy weeds
are frozen and don't sway at all
in the light wind
the milkweed look an anemic
and sickly bird of paradise very far from home

in those fields
pressed into the snow in outline
are the wings the heads the bodies
of a flock of wild turkeys
the impression is white on white
some wild turkey winter ritual
or it just felt so good
to roll in that soft quiet snow

this morning began
not like those turkeys
it began like ancient oak trees

bare branches spreading in all directions
like the sad eyes of some shepherd dog
it began with too much morning sun

driving north along the palisades
the middle of february
and winter still hasn't fully arrived
every other day or two
all living things are tricked
into thinking it's spring again

driving north along the palisades
the same owl is perched thirty feet up
its still its eyes are fixed
waiting for breakfast or
still waiting for last night's dinner
its breast fluffed
and waiting too for february

the sun starts to fade and
that wonderfully faint pungent odor of skunk
enters the car
and travels with me for awhile

above state line
a red tail hawk drops out of the sky
and lands on the right edge of the right lane

its wings spread
like the cape of bela lugosi
its head bent into the wind
coming off the river
about to change someone's life forever

in the rear and side mirrors
i see it hardly move
as a slower moving car in that lane
passes only inches to its left

at 11 the sun has half disappeared
there's talk of snow
and you can feel the weather
coming inside clearing out
any lingering smell of skunk

thirty miles north
the sun has gone
leaving a hot white spot
behind the slowly thickening clouds
coming from the north and from the west
as speculations move in the opposite direction

by now that owl has eaten
the hawk has finished feeding
and the skunk
in all likelihood will never eat again

forty minutes later
it's colder and the grayness
that forms the world before it snows
is all around me
                    as i feel you are now
as close as i am to myself
driving north to meet the ones i love

Eating Lunch

we're eating lunch
about 3:30 after a late breakfast
and some hard garden work
just something quick to eat
outside under the sunshine
it being the first sunny day
in a week or two

above us two hawks are
circling and looking for their lunch

we eat leisurely have coffee
and something sweet to make it complete

the two hawks are still circling
not yet having had any luck

Then and Now
June '67-June '05

1

so rummy how's that back door draft coming
along? you ought to talk to bob mcnamara. he
tried something similar in sixty-seven. low on
troops. 500,000 still low on troops. he figured i
guess 50,000 more would certainly help. put the
north on the run. call in the reservists who were
not reserving no matter what the reason.
activate them all that'll put the north on the run
…and kellogg brown and root were there too.
right in the thick of it as usual.

2
it's spring now
and it was spring in 1967
when mcnamara and congress
                              adjusted the law
so we left
              stewart and me
                              with our dogs
for montreal before
the bureaucracy could get going
nine months later
when our time was up
we left for vancouver

the two of us stewart's wife to be and
of course the dogs

we followed the highway out of montreal
to toronto and down to detroit
to avoid the canadian snow

some minor trouble with immigration
then to morehead minnesota
where the ice flipped the car over 360 degrees
no damage but the tires were shot
then fargo...
                    the next day into montana
the snow started to fall

3

no real plan in vietnam rummy no plan here.
well anyway rummy you you can't hurt me you
or your bosses. but you do upset me terribly
with your edition of the rendition rag abu
ghraib maher arar and on and on. really donny
who did plan this one? it's always the same
people isn't it? people who don't plan for the
full consequences only the political moment
and the economic and financial dreams.
eisenhower didn't think kennedy johnson nixon
didn't think even ronnie reagan didn't think
interfering with the soviets and their afgan
troubles supplying training the future jihadists.

just couldn't let the soviets fall apart on their
own.

you donny and georgie and paulie pearl condi
chaney firth addington you all should have
known better. you're supposed to be
somebodies. i knew better and i'm nobody. so
where does that leave you?

4

around midnight we stopped in livingston
the only place open for miles
it was quiet the snow falling
                              no trucks
just us and one waitress
                         maybe two
we ate and talked
the three of us…and jody

after an hour we left
about five miles out of town
                              the snow stops
stewart and carol and the dogs are asleep
mr tambourine is on the radio
i can hear just for a second
the sound of her wave

next thing
           we're sinking into the shoulder
up to a foot of snow

everyone's awake now
out of the car
                    and lennie the big male dog
takes off after the bark of a dog
across a desolate field
there's nothing to do
nowhere to go...
                    luck again
the highway crew is out and
although they weren't supposed to
they pulled us out
we had taken the wrong road...
                              closed in winter
back in the car
it was uneventful through idaho and
most of washington state

vancouver...
                    a nice city then maybe
you could get out of town into the hills
maybe fifteen minutes
the cops of course
were the same as in most places

stewart and carol left for san francisco
and on a warm beautiful day
lennie and me started driving east
following the border

the farther east
the more the clouds formed

the colder it got
then the snow
and more snow until
we were stopped in trail bc
two days in a blizzard
with singing canaries in the small
 hotel coffee shop

5

again donny. what do you know about human
nature? about sending soldiers to fight "dead
enders" who did nothing to us except they
happen to be sitting on a large pool of oil. you
impose a false personalization on those soldiers
while those dead enders do have a real and
personal stake in the matter. you can keep that
up for just so long. 2004 george is on top. says
he has a mandate . six months later the mandate
is gone. but you all keep on with the same
defiant shitspeak attitude as if it were the
reality.

6

when the weather cleared we
passed through the immigration point
at porthill idaho
talked about dogs
with the immigration officer
and the chinese made

16

flannel shirt i had on

we followed the road to bonners ferry
and sandpoint
              then to missoula
following the clark fork river

i'm comfortable in the front seat
with my heater
lennie is sprawled out in the back

we stop by the tracks in whithall
                              and sleep

breakfast in manhattan montana
                              near the tracks
the cowboys walk in
another old movie set

7

i get into livingston at night
check into a motel
and spend the next two days eating in the diner
no sign of jody

finally i ask a waitress
and on my third day in livingston
i have dinner after midnight

we don't say much to each other

on my way out
my stomach slides back down into itself
into a warm blue place
as she hands me the keys
and directions to her apartment

8

donny i believe you and your bosses are one of
the worst administrations this country has ever
had. you have the capacity to become fully
fledged fascists in the name of saving us from
the ills of the outer world in the belief that we
are now and forever in harm's way. and you
made iran one of your evil axi richer a more
important middle east player and more able to
cause more trouble than if you had done
nothing. at the very least you could have tried
to talk it up with them. after all the shah was
our fault and so the ayatollahs become our fault
too. oil again…

9

i bring my things up
along with lennie
                    to the top floor
of a three story house and
it's comfortable there
in small town montana

i can't sleep

at six jody comes home
and we talk for awhile

from the window
we look out to the court house below
the quiet empty streets and
to the snow covered mountains

                              north of town

it was not your good looks
it was your look
and as complicated
                    or as simple
as the sound of your wave

its lasted a lifetime

                    10

we woke that first morning
walked around town
talked to a few people
had breakfast
                    walked some more
                              and talked

i drove jody to work

had dinner
came home and slept

when jody came home
we talked slept and
driving into the country that afternoon
felt good
we began to settle into each other

the road to yellowstone was closed for the
winter

11

i'm here for about a week
everything seems okay or so i think
i talk to the old men
who sit in chairs on main street
who no longer seem interested
in politics or religion

we talk about dogs and
i get along with most
of the younger people
who no longer belong there

a little after midnight
i pick up jody

driving home

i get an odd feeling behind me
suddenly the flashing lights are on
two locals and the highway patrol
and although it may seem trivial now
their attempt at intimidation
                                    was not
their top lights whirling

12

i pull over
was i speeding? no
-hello jody
jody says hello
-can i see your license and registration?
                                    real nice and polite
-sure was i speeding?
-no
he goes back to the other two cars
and they look at the car
and talk
and look
-you've got till tomorrow morning to get over
to the court house get montana plates on the car
-oh?
-you born in canada or the states?
-new york
-what were you doing in canada?
- i was working in montreal
-can i see your draft card?
-it's at home

-that's illegal you know

                              pronounced as if the united
                                 states were in the middle
                                     of a world war and
                              espionage was everywhere

-yeah but i'm finished with that
and all the while lennie
is barking in the back seat
trying to get out of the window
-you go get your papers
an bring them over to the station house
                                    all nice and polite
then the highway guy
steps up front
tells me again about the plates

they follow us
i get "the papers" and
follow them back to their house and
into the talk it over room
                              just like the movies

they look at the papers
ask a few questions
make a few notes
                     i thought it was a slow night
but it wasn't

then it comes

                     the predecessors of
                                        james dobson
                                        pat robertson
                                        the tailiban
                                        tom delay
                                        fallwell
                                        iranian
                                        ayatollas
                                        rick santorum
the religious of mass destruction
unlike the weapons
are always with us

-where are you living james?
i tell them with jody
-yeah that's the report we got
report? what report to myself
-you married james?
                     all chummy on a first name basis
-no
-jody's not married neither huh james?
-no not that i know of
i sort of hum to myself
-we don't go for that sort of thing around here
james
that's a criminal act carries a sentence of five
years
and a $500 fine
-i didn't know that
-well now you do see that you act accordingly
-you can go now

they were all too nice and polite
like evil in the movies
the same red lights whirling
outside of the police house and
my stomach is slipping away again
this is not a joyful anticipatory slippage

13

and still 2005 may 13th on the radio a sheriff in
small town north carolina tells his newly hired
dispatcher she either marries her boy friend or
finds separate living accommodations or she's
fired. he says she's in violation of an 1805 anti-
cohabitation law and it was not only a criminal
act it was also morally offensive. according to
the news most legal scholars believe the law is
unconstitutional.

14

next morning
i don't trust the only lawyer in town

finally in a small corner of missoula
i get advice from a law professor
-they're full of shit kid
but it's a small town
they'll get you if they want

i rent the second floor
we have a duplex
and that's the end of that

15

we talked and talked
ulcers at eighteen
-i wish i were jewish
i think i saw moses on the day i was born

jody grew up in livingston
among the mountains

too gentle against all the snow and wind
from livingston to bozmon then berkeley and
flagstaff

-i wish i were jewish

married for three months at seventeen
a few more escapes
then back to livingston
-i had a horse when i was young
and road bareback through the snow

she carried an aura of a slightly
failed innocence…a vulnerability

-i too easily become what others are

it was 1968
it was very easy very comfortable
for both of us

16

after awhile
jody had to stop working
we were both sick

first the doctor blamed jody
then me but
it was his bad medicine
                              sometime earlier

we couldn't get served
in any restaurant in the county
                                        not even coffee

17

jody wanted to leave
she had to leave
get away from the people she
had known all her life
go to missoula become anonymous

i couldn't go
not then
there were things i had to do in new york

26

before i could do anything else

18

i left on a monday
i moved some of jody's things
to the train station

we said good-bye at the post office
it was a little like dying
when that's not at all
                  what you had in mind

i remember giving you a telephone number
that you could always call
you had none to give me

you never called

two three months later
i could find no trace of you

by the time i reached worden
                      150 miles east
the temperature had climbed to eighty

19

i look at the maps and
see booneville missouri
i remember eating chili

four years earlier
during a blizzard
and a motel in sweet springs
the pink motel

chicago the lincoln highway
all the way into new york city
thinking of sad jody

you had no number to give
you never called

20

the law is donny that ignorance of the law is no
excuse and just as correct your lack of
understanding of history your arrogance donny
none of it lets you or your bosses off the world
view hook. you and your mob have created this
untenable event and all you can do to correct it
is to make it worse. and all the while the
jihadists still dream of creating their own
tsunami off the coast of maine.

21

on april 17th of this year
a hot sunny sunday i
called again and still no you

i pulled out the atlas...

                            and there

i never called in 1968
or thirty minutes ago

                           unlisted they said

but there

i hope you're happy
at least comfortable
and no one else has harmed you

at least comfortable
and as anonymous as you want

Elsie Talk got Elsie into Trouble

the messages come in daily
elsie talk sprawled across the page
and in between the type
explanations neatly worked

the messages come faster
faster with a fever
love notes
to con ed
to ma bell
to the social security administration
to the landlord
elsie's love notes to the world

later in the office elsie smiles
when she thinks of the eight years in hospital
and to elsie now is then
the talk is all the same

calls are made

in the taxi elsie smokes and squints her eyes
i think of a chiffon pie

somehow we manage to make it in one piece
before the sounds start running from her mouth
the dama dama die gie
as she grabs my hand
like a child

holding tight
moving faster
dama dama faster to the door

inside dr graham
feels elsie needs a rest
so she can stop
the talking in her head
she's 54
and loves her home
for what it's worth
but the doctor
knows the score the law
and just about everything else
as they lead elsie away

on my way out
i pass elsie in the waiting room
strapped into an old
wooden wheel chair
shot with thorazine
looking like the quietest sparrow
the dama dama stopped
elsie stopped

as i pass
i touch her head and smile

she tries to smile back
but it comes out like crushed velvet

Driving Along Route 30

driving along route 30 northbound
around the pepaction reservoir
in mid-state new york
going 40
a little overcast but clear

suddenly on a straightaway
a young deer a doe
several months old
runs from the right
i slam the breaks
the car doesn't swerve
and neither does the deer

she hits my right front end
flies backwards hits the asphalt
and lies there stunned

i come to a stop thirty feet away
put on the disaster lights and wait

from my point of view it's the tail i notice
it doesn't seem to be
where it should be

i wait

she begins to struggle
to drag herself off the road

into the cool grass
using her chin to pull herself forward
in a slow and deliberate way

i slowly walk towards her
when i'm three feet away
she begins to scream
the most terrible and frightened scream
i back off and wait

one or two cars pass and move
around her slowly
a woman stops
says she'll stop again at a house up the road
they've got a gun there she says

i wait

two ladies stop
driving the same car as mine
ask if i'm alright...car running?
i tell them yes i'm waiting for the gun to arrive
a guy stops says he usually carries a pistol

but not today

finally a fisherman in a van pulls off the road
he comes out with a filleting knife
and without any hesitation
he puts the knife
into the side of the deer's throat

he makes several cuts
and the deer is gone
just like that

all of her guts are hanging out
the spot on the road is ruined
crushed and destroyed forever

the eyes are open wide
staring up at me
her body still very warm
when i touch her side and say good-bye

the throat slitter grabs her ear
and drags her off into that cool grass
very all business very efficient
very good at what he had to do
and blaming the environmentalists
the anti-hunting crowd for this death
because there are too many deer
and right at that moment
his point could be taken
in a strange reversal of things

Saved by the Israeli Army

it had been going on for some time
evil eyes everywhere hexes
all kinds of bad luck signs
even the dog looking at me in a strange way
women too
it's no wonder
i'm a little unsure
about dinner
with two old people i know
and their niece from the israeli army
suffering from culture shock

later when me and the soldier
go back to get the dog
there's mail from out west
they thank me say
they can't use the poems at this time
they're very polite

even the israeli is polite
which is at least better than it was yesterday

January 2003

driving on one of the smaller roads
in the northern catskills
on a bleak cold and damp day
it feels like a new year's day
a long time ago in montreal
a damp and absolutely deadening day
in montreal in 1979

now perched on the wall
of a deserted foundation
that once was going to be
someone's small home
two black cats
watching us pass

Passing the Time of Day

passing through all those houses
and sometimes into all those houses
seeing all the shit
man inflicts upon himself
and all the shit
he has inflicted upon him
from this one and that one
from strangers and from lovers and friends
and dealing with all the diseases
incurable and otherwise
all the madnesses
the plagues the fires
the floods the floods of every kind
you think somehow
it's going to prepare you
for when it comes home to visit

but it doesn't

Life is so much more than Eating Crow

it's the crow that marks the spot
and it's always a wonderful day for a crow dream

doesn't every crow you know
contain
pennies from heaven

or try crow for a day
or one good crow deserves another

stella by crow light
is not a dream
so don't throw
your crows at me
people will say
we're in love

and if I could crow with you
one hour a day
i would have you
under my crow

then
suddenly it's spring again
the crows on the wing again

therefore
to thine own crow be true

and what a difference
a crow will make to you

it truly is a wonderful world
for the crow
having all of the reverence
                              from some
and none of the responsibility of the eagle

so just wrap your troubles in crow
and crow your troubles away

Everybody's Luck Runs Out

between her 1940's 1950's good looks
standing with her husband
arms around each other
at some seaside resort in an old
black and white photo
dressed in what was then
smart casual clothing posing
for the camera
and her present state of affairs at 96
with her right side the
whole of it in constant pain
her legs swollen
alone except for the hired help
help hired by other people
whom she cannot tolerate
and her needing night time
and morning time treatments
her money running out her
power of attorney trying to
run her into a nursing home

between all that
she did have a wonderful life

Everybody's Tears

this elderly woman has a phd
she taught history at columbia

this elderly woman
is retired now
and she's ill
and the cure
has taken her dignity
more than the cancer
which would have taken her life

she opens the door
dressed in a navy blue blouse
a very nice blouse
and an adult diaper

we sit
we talk
there are things i have to do for her
things to arrange and re-arrange
just to keep the place and her going
she's anxious very anxious
she hears very little that i say
so i have to repeat
everything 5, 6, 7 times
and i'm starting to get annoyed
the questions keep coming
they keep coming yet
somehow it all seems to get settled

as i'm leaving
standing at the door
she can no longer hold back the tears
and the fact
that last week
she took all the pills she could find
and only slept
for a very long time

when she woke
the diaper needed
to be changed several diapers ago
i was a professor she says
i was a person
now look at me
all i want is to die
and the tears get worse

usually i take this in stride
i'm able to smooth it over for awhile
i don't think there's a safe way out
for this professor

but just now
seeing her
seeing the tears
seeing the diaper
just now
the indignity of it all
is too much

i can hardly hold back
my tears
before walking out through that door

Everybody's Tears Just Stopped

i get a call from the phd
she's screaming into the phone
and her homeless son
is screaming in the background
when you were here she says
you made me sign something
what was it
i explain it to her
very quietly very calmly
well i don't want it
i want what i have now
again i explain
if you don't take what we will give you
they will take from you what you now have
it's the switch it's very simple
they stop we start
no way around it i'm sorry
well i don't want it she says
i want what i have
and we dance through it two more times

your medicaid i tell her
we changed it
now you can use it all the time
you won't have to spend the excess first
excess to the state
real money to her
if i want to spend my money she says
that's my business

that expensive medicine i tell her
medicaid will pay for it
no they won't she says
yes they will i tell her
well if i want to pay for it
that's what i want
i want what i have now
you caught me at a bad moment
when you were here
i was very sick
now i'm filled with all of these pills
that nurse you sent
i don't want her here
and so on and so on and so on

i speak to some people
who speak to her and
i speak to her again
at first she sounds reasonable
she just walked in
she has to take off her clothes
she has to use the toilet
she's all over the apartment
and from wherever she is she's
talking at the phone to me
hold on i'll be there
and like that for five minutes

now she's back and
whatever reasonableness there was is gone

and we're back to
i want what i have
even if i can't have it

my only chance is yes
yes to whatever it is she wants
yes to whatever it is she says
yes yes yes
and yes we end the conversation
very pleasantly
very civil
she even thanks me

however we will do what
we were going to do

she may not be incompetent
but that does not give her the right
to allow us to destroy her

Only a Few Body Parts Remain

only a few body parts remain
in the parking area at the east river
where the police sometimes at dusk
really do practice
handling confrontation
but you know that neither side
will pull the loaded gun on the other
and neither side will really know
the anger and the fear
in that one waiting confrontation
until it comes

until recently
that parking area held
all of the crushed cars
after the lawn on grand street collapsed
much as the police practice does
in day light or in night light
collapsed right into the parking garage below
destroying just about everything down there

the sea gulls gleaming and white
making squawking sea gull sounds
in the late day march sun
pass over the sparkling water flying scared
or so it seems
because of the mallard duck couple diving for fish

the sea gulls pick at those remains
the same as the quiet people
who live under the blue tarp
in a corner of the chinese park on essex street
with all their belongings
and only their dogs
for warmth and some comfort...pick

even their dogs are quiet
in those not so spare living arrangements
and even the police
                        for now leave them alone

Mathew Brady Loves his Fruit

i come across something one day
about mathew brady
photographs of mathew brady
photographs by mathew brady
other pictures and books
concerning the sociology of mathew brady
and while my back is turned he disappears
swallowed up in the darkness
gone with all his belongings
losing himself in the wind
sold out his stock
and left with the weather

i figure i won't see him again
smiling and nodding to people
his fingers extended in a gesture
lighting candles
looking into garbage heaps
dusting off something he likes
and slipping it into one of the satchels
strapped to his back

he's gone and time passes
i go on listening
to the rustle of the leaves

the months pass
and suddenly he's back with the spring
atop a pile of wooden crates
moonlit
mysteriously eating a fruit
and smiling like harry lime

All Night at the Greengrocers

while i'm rubbing the fuzz
on the peaches
5 californians hop out
and ask the little guy
with the bum arm
about the grapes

he says something
about arizona
but they bust up the place anyway
and drive off shouting at me
say they know who i am
where i live

the cops come
and lennie an me go
to search out mathew brady
nestled into his box bed
in a doorway
with candles in his eyes

mathew is eating his fruit as usual
there's nothing left for us
so he just smiles
and because the smell is june
i'm ready for another go at 7th street

the valencias are dripping
only this time behind us quick

this guy coming smells of nothing good
but the cop behind him does
and it's up against the glass wall
hung with kielbasy and hams
and the cop wants the guy's gun

in between the screaming
about civil rights
about discrimination
a cab stops
a bus stops
a truck stops
and 10 cop cars stop
so the guy stops
and gives up the gun
everyone seems genuinely happy

everyone except the guy with the gun
who still wants to walk
and the little guy with the bum arm
who is ready to cry
cause it's such a beautiful night
the fruit is ripe
it smells like heaven
but nobody's buying

Love and the Weather don't always work out

it's gray outside
it's 6am
in the kitchen
i've been up all night
wrestling with the one i love
and it hasn't been fun
i'm tired and there are
things i have to do soon

it's 6 and the snow is falling
in the air shaft
bending a small pine tree
it's become a snow tree
soft and asleep till spring

we've been running in a fugue
i have my life
she has my life
she has her life
but doesn't know the way

the talk goes on
with all its connotations
and all the variations
and we come to conclusions
only we don't come to conclusions
so we talk
and talk is tired

the snow falling
everything going to sleep

i get up
through the kitchen
into a hotel room in buenos aires
it's august
it's a strange city
the snow is falling
and i don't know the name
of the girl in my bed
she looks like a french starlet
with pouting lips
and a camel's hair coat

she can't speak english
i don't speak spanish
and we get along just the same

in the kitchen
it's still 6am and snowing
we're all exhausted
even the dog
and he hasn't said anything

there are no birds outside
only our tongues stretching the air
the snow piling up

music like this
i need to be
surrounded by snow
not able to speak
naked and warm in the snow

If you can Afford a Maid, Maybe

urena is a small lady
a bird lady
she's not deadly
this displaced lady
living alone on mott street
but the neighbors do think she's odd
that's why they send me out
to see her at home
to get the feel of it
and that's why i bring her back
to see the doctor in his home
so he can get the feel of it

urena used to be a cleaning lady
big office buildings
late at night
that sort of thing
till a car hit her in '72
and then took off

all the bones have healed
at least that's what the doctors say

she still cleans up a bit
mopping the halls with kerosene
which leaves plenty of time
for her to burn the bones
to re-arrange the black beans and clam shells
then with the touch of a julia child

a little orange peel curled around the dish
which leaves plenty of time
for her to wrap her head
in old paper and old rags
to stop the pain she says
which the doctors say has disappeared

she wraps the rags carefully
making a long train she carries
like mott street royalty
which all leaves plenty of time
for her to entertain and fight
but this distracts her and
the water overflows

when i take her to see the doctor
we find out what the real problem is
why she burns the bones
and burns the kerosene
it's the chinese she says
it's the japanese
in the cellar
it's the machines they operate down there
the machines that make the toilets flush
and the walls are like a sponge

she says these people are not after her
and they only like to have fun
but they are dangerous
and they will kill you
and they will eat you up

the doctor shakes his head
he agrees
the chinese
the japanese he says
i'd burn bones too he says
but her judgment is impaired as well
chronic he says
even with treatment
she's unlikely to significantly improve
in the near future
bring in protective services he says
even if we can't stop the machines
after all we're not plumbers
we can at least clean up the water
when the sponges are full

Fifty-Fifty

it's about noon when i arrive
last weeks dishes
still in the sink

i can hardly move
among his things between his chaos
his audio tapes and video tapes
the painted canvases his
musical instruments the three bikes
one on the wall
the other two leaning against broken chairs and
audio equipment belonging to several audio
systems
plastic bags on the floor
bits of paper crumbs
scraps of everything everywhere

and there's a cat
long haired gray and white
she's a very sweet long haired cat
he says he rescued her from another
apartment in the building
where she was being tormented by two dogs

now the torment is all around her

he's half dressed now and very slow
he's half reclining on the bed
in his half clothes telling me
he has metal in his back
pins screws strips of metal flat hinges
a spinal fusion and he's still in pain

it's very warm in there and
damp all the windows closed
secure against what may be waiting outside
and with global warming
the chances of mutation
at least in there
are fairly good
so he expects those termites
will get him before god does

seeing him move with that pain
i hope he's right

High Noon

i'm watching the girl
with the skinny ribbed sweater
coming towards me on 13th street

it' s spring and sunny
and she has on shoes
that show her feet
her breasts are moving nicely

the carpenter comes out of his shop
and also watches
as she passes the both of us
and walks on
we both look at each other and smile

it's nice to know
that you're not alone at lunchtime
in the spring
when everything is alive

I Get a Call from Back There

i get a call from back there

larry died
your uncle larry died this afternoon

it feels flat

we were never close
he wasn't my uncle
he was my mother's uncle

i last saw him 6 months ago
before he went in for surgery

before that
we hadn't seen each other in several years
he didn't recognize me

there were nine sisters and brothers
each stranger than the other

now there's only two left
and they don't speak

we were never really close
but he's dead now
this same day
and it all seems very flat

my closest hands are old enough to die
and there will be funerals to take care of

i would rather they die
and become vapor

i don't want funerals
and chapels for them
and people saying things

then the weeping
everyone being sorry

my mother when she goes
should just as suddenly
become a daisy
and my father
a big spreading geranium
thick and green
and always with at least one red blossom
standing beyond all the other plants
                                    in the garden

Louise Didly Calls my Name in the Night
and when she's well she runs the chuck a luck game on 3rd street

for 12 years louise has been coming & going
between her 6th floor walk-ups
and bellevue & manhattan state hospitals
and somewhere else i'll never know

the first time i met louise
she was nailed to the floor
gripping her fingers and rocking
her eyes locked on the window sill
and i was a christ dripping with water
coming up through the floor boards
with an arm full of fish
she should have been in queens
visiting her youngest child
but it's so hard to move
when you can't
and you're very far away

on the other hand
when louise feels sexy
she's hot she's burning up
and has to rip off all her clothes
on the roof at the market
in the streets
wherever she is because
she's hot because she feels very sexy

and what visions
pass through her mind
no mere mortal can ever know

it's difficult to do much for louise
sometimes we talk and there are
strange apartments she wants to take me to
with animal sounds
these are not places that i can go to
but i will share the macaroni salad
she pulls from her hair
like the wizard of the kitchen
and when she's lost her eyes
i will lead her carefully down the stairs
to the wagon below
waiting to take her to heaven

"Every Time We Say Goodbye"

it was so comfortable
that warm winter saturday
the two of us and the dog
bundled and nestled between the rocks
of that rock jetty
on the jersey side of the hudson
the palisades above
the sky blue brilliant the water brilliant
the view clear to the bottom of manhattan
and betty carter
brilliant

Morton Sobell's Other Mother

i get the referral on rosie
eyesight going
earshot going
organic brain syndrome
may be the only thing that's coming

she's 82 last july
and i figure
it's just another older woman
needs a little help
maybe she's got a son
a daughter maybe
take care of her on weekends
and we'll do the rest

when i get there
she greets me at the door
with the latest copy of the daily world
very glad to see me
didn't think i'd make it in the rain
only what i've got worked out
isn't what rosie's worked out
homemaker is fine she says
anything i want
is okay with her
only it's her son morton
still alive after 18 years in jail
still alive after rosie's tramped
all over the world preaching

still alive after being one of the best engineers
and such a kind boy
and still alive
after the rosenbergs are dead
still alive and living on the upper west side
still alive
but you couldn't swear to it by rosie

Song for a One Legged Typist

mostly though i come
with an armful of legal pads
and as i hit the door
drop down on one knee
and give out with a chorus of "angel eyes"

i think it's pretty good
although the neighbors don't
and toss their cats in the hall

but if the world
should suddenly come to an end
through the misdeeds
of all the big shots
or if it should just as suddenly
decide to give up on its own
tired of us all
i do hope i can quietly
slip with her
into the olivetti

Knowing You Never Eat Breakfast

knowing you never eat breakfast
after leaving in the morning
i stop for coffee and something sweet

sitting in the window
watching people rushing to work
i'm in no rush
even the cigarette smoke of strangers
doesn't bother me

i'd forgotten the feeling
of lying next to you all night
and the wonderful ordinariness of waking
and finding you
still there

Spring 2003

high up
on the ides of march
we see the first geese flying home
the sky is terribly blue
and there's still two feet of snow
on the mountain

i was never so happy to see the geese
after such a winter joan says

it had been snowing
every three or four days
the access road to the house
getting more and more narrow
so that at one point
a "bobcat" had to be hired
to widen it before
it closed completely
and the driveway
also lost some of itself

even the plowman was unable to perform
although with more than several children
with several women
you wonder what happened
was it him or the weather

even he needed assistance two times
to become 'disengaged'
from the snow banks
he had previously made
leaving us with numerous
six by six by six inch holes
in the ice-snow surface

time passes
and in late april it snowed again

on the first of may as usual
the "spring beauties" are out
and some little snow
is still on the slopes
where we find ourselves
after taking a short cut
across a hill

the place is deserted
the lift chairs have been put to sleep
only the dogs and
the two of us

we walk to the bottom
sit in the almost
                    warm grass
and give the iraqi shoe
to the last of this winter

After Mailing a Letter

after mailing a letter
at 57th and eighth avenue
i'm waiting for the light to change
it's 6:30 pm
96 degrees
crowded
and one of the two pretty woman
goes in to work the atm machine
the one wearing the
very gauzy white pants
waits outside
me i would have gone inside
for the air conditioning
and to escape the ozone alert
but she'd rather wait
in the heat
in those very gauzy pants
that give the very real appearance
of nothing underneath all that gauziness

most of the traffic
is too far away to notice
and the sidewalk traffic
is just too close
and too hot to see beyond itself

but the two motorcycles
running in the very right lane
hugging the curb
                almost collide
over all that gauze
all that gauze

The Gem of 4th Street

when jennie left the hospital
all the social workers
felt sorry for jennie
she'd been living freestyle
feeding the cats uptown
collecting garbage
and collecting a little social security
she'd been collecting things for years
until she was hit on the head
and all the social workers thought
jennie ought to have a home
a place of her own
i know it's not going to work
but what the hell
if it's not this it'll be something else
so we get jennie a place
not good but not bad either
she fixes herself up with a bed
from somewhere
and all the social workers think
isn't that great
on her own
she got a bed on her own
all except me of course
i think it's just another piece
she's pulled off the street
and then we get dollars
to buy all kinds of things

only i can never find jennie at home
the only time i do see jennie
is at 2 in the morning
on 1st avenue when i'm walking the dog
her shopping bags are filled
looking for her uptown cats
for 4 months i'm trying
to get jennie at home
and after 4 months
she tells me on 1st avenue
at 2 in the morning
she's stopped paying the rent
the refrigerator stopped working
she lost two kosher chickens
and the landlord won't fix it
i tell her she'd better pay the rent
or she'll wind up with the chickens
she says yes
but i know she won't
i can tell she's ready to fight

two weeks later
she's still not home
the door is open
and i can see jennie's
been fixing up the place
and if all the social workers in the city
had been there
they might not have thought it was so great
and no wonder she's never home
too busy fixing up the place

wall to wall garbage
3 feet high
3 rooms of it
and no wonder the refrigerator won't work
and no wonder the landlord won't fix it
but her bed is still there
the gem of 4th street
a spread on the bed
very neat
three cats sleeping
three cats as fat as pigs
by this time i know jennie's had it

soon the marshall is there
out he says
that's it out
and she won't go to a shelter
and i can't blame her for that
so she sleeps in doorways
tormented by children until they scoop her up
cart her off to queens general
then it's back out on the street
back to the doorways and the torment
this time all the social workers in the city
aren't taking any chances
this time it's a rest home in queens
near the sea
and if she's lucky
she'll just rest there
for the next 30 years

The Grand Standers

the end of march
and the crows
are talking
        more than ever

nearly the end of may
and the bluejays
        are still crowing
causing no confusion

Airport Letter

it's december
and that mushroom in your head
is getting bigger
everything tightening up again
not quite steel yet

but it doesn't matter anymore
i love you

it's not quite the way it was though
in the spring
when you were full of joy
and the world was in love

i brought you birds of paradise
and calla lillies
and everything was clear

then it all changed
you wanted nothing
less than nothing
everything was still clear though
then it all changed again
and then again
each time everything was clear
each frame different but just as clear
each frame different
but just as real

only a breath
in the right or wrong place

we have learned about each other
in spite of all the different frames
we have learned from each other

last night i brought you a bird of paradise
and a eucalyptus branch
set it on the shelf over your head
to look after you while i'm away i said
and your laugh
was real and warm for awhile

today overnight
you seemed to have dropped one notch
waiting for tom swift
and what talk there was
was more of an effort
for both of us

the walk home
was mostly in silence
that goodbye sounded like death

in a few hours i'll be in california
to gather up the sun for you
here is a quarter of a million
in flight insurance
which if i should die en route
never again to lay my head

between those shimmering glass thighs
will at least pay
for a new yugoslavian pony
to replace the one that was stolen
so you can ride out on the pier at sunset
and watch it quietly for the both of us

At Last There's a Place for the Garbage

the little guy is dead
burned himself up
all 100 pounds
smoking in bed
the rest of the building along with himself

all day he'd walk
up and down the block
back and forth
muttering to himself in spanish
yelling at the landlord he worked for
to get more trash cans
get more cans he'd scream
                              at old hungry face
there's no room for all this crap

he was genuinely concerned
this little guy
who muttered to himself

all the makings of a fine citizen

but one night he falls asleep
his cigarette going
and wakes up in flames
                      too late
he and the building are d o a

the landlord
                old hungry face
tins up the windows
but the junkies come
and the kids come
and tear down the tin
and live in there for awhile
making more fires to keep warm

they soon get tired of it all
                        and leave
but the rest of the block
they know a good thing when they see it
and of course
                old hungry
                        is happy
he doesn't have to lay out
for those extra cans

The Peacock

my wife and i are
walking the girls on 10th avenue
and we meet up
with this very large
         and very handsome pitbull

his owner although not dressed
like a peacock
         struts like one

the bull starts sniffing the girls
         and they him

i say to the peacock
         he's in heaven

the peacock is expressionless
         and says nothing

i say he's a male isn't he?
         the peacock looks

two girls i say he's in heaven
the peacock, expressionless,
tells me he has seven girl friends
as if it matters to dogs
and my wife, expressionless,
stifles a laugh
that lasts for three blocks

Everyone Wants to Get into the Act

i make one of my usual calls
on the third floor
in the rear
i find israel ayala and his wife
he's been drinking some five star special
his face half eaten away

israel and his wife
seven months pregnant
sleep on the floor
they have
no money
no clothes
no food

he takes another slug
and i feel his
brain candle start to flutter
i ask him what's this
you've got nothing here
the place looks like a sty
he says they've been like this
since israel smashed his wrist
and lost his job
and just as the flame is about to go out
that jesus too slept on the floor

During the First Week of June

during the first week of june
when there was no more chance of frost
we planted eight pots of pansies

they were beautiful as pansies are
multi colored healthy looking
and seemed to hold such promise
there in the center of the garden
promise like my mother daisy's cousin pansy
who went south for the weather
opened a flower shop
and as the business expanded
she grew smaller

as time passed these pansies too
have had trouble with too much rain
and into the end of july
they still looked healthy
still multi colored but
now half their original size

come next june
we'll try again
pansy never got that chance

Driving Across the Brooklyn Bridge

driving across the brooklyn bridge
listening to dinah washington
i come to tillery street
it looks like school has let out
or they walked out in protest
walking in all directions shouting
i wonder if they'll ever know who she was

i continue south to the park
some of my mother's and father's ashes
on the seat next to me

the major portion of those ashes
are in a sealed urn
sitting in my closet
my sister who held them
and still wants to hold them
will get them back when she gets back

she finds comfort in having them around
having had so many loses of her own
i don't
who were my mother and father
are still inside of me
not in that beautiful urn

still knowing my sister
those ashes will hang around

till her own ashes emerge
in some closet
and while they may not be
who they once were
i don't want all of what's left
to be emptied along
with her lifetime's accumulation

the park the lake the flora
around the edge of the lake
is full and summer green

a slight breeze moves the water

there are some ducks
the males and the females are
getting no breaks from each other

at the edge of the shore
i slip the ashes out of the plastic bag
stir them into the water
and watch the ducks acting
not unlike the rest of us

i eat an apple
keep their memory even stronger
as i watch the ashes move on
to the place where they first met

Caught in the Line of Fire

my grandmother is dying now
ten years of cancer and
how her throat growls
since the stroke
                and says nothing

once she was full faced
had the most beautiful skin
now she has hollows in her head
no useful legs no teeth

she lies in bed all day
she worries about the man
who comes for the real estate
and my grandmother
who was never quite the joker
asks my other aunt
to remove the ship from under her arm

                ----
you see
           he's too funny now
wants to be the man he never was
while my other aunt
is dying of cancer

uncle dan says
you people never tell me anything
just let me know

i'm a very very rich man

so my other aunt sends letters
and finally calls
tells uncle dan
she's going in for a transfusion tomorrow
uncle dan says
he's going to london too
and tells my other aunt
                              to have a good trip

Entering the Buddhist Temple

entering the buddhist temple
on lafayette street
snug between a manufacturer of parts
a cheap art gallery
a qi gong massage and back rub store front
and a chinese fish dealer selling live
in tanks fresh water shrimp

i walk past the pews and alter
to the room in back
where food is prepared

when i arrive lunch has been over
for at least an hour
                        so i'm offered fruit

i speak for awhile with one of the nuns
she explains the priest's condition
i have papers from his doctor
it's a 24 hour job to care for him
they all have other work to do

we go upstairs to his living quarters
i nod my head in his direction
he puts his hands tip to tip
bows slightly and says nothing

i fill in some forms make some observations
and with the help of yin lee

ask a few questions
he answers but basically
goes about his own business
watching a video screen and its images

he does have a religious aura about him
and just slightly his mind
is beginning to move away from itself
he still is able to give the impression
of someone
who believes he has done everything right
lost all desires

will he be back ?
i'm sure he believes
                    he will not

Waiting for the Traffic at St Marks Place

after 15 years she said
stripping was the only thing she knew
and there were 3 kids to support
told me she had a breakdown once
maybe 7, 8 yrs ago
said she'd like to really go insane
just be left to sit in a rocker
and look out at nothing
said she had trouble reading shakespeare & wilde
but liked poe very much
that stripping was more than just a g string an tits
and would i please buy her a bottle of champagne

Traffic Control

i take them to the hospitals
to the psychiatric hospitals
i take them home
to mothers
to fathers
i take them home to their children
to shelters
old age homes
even to their own homes
with the rats & bugs to look after them
when its dark
i take them to all the places
you don't want to take them to

and even though i know
there's nothing out there
or up there
where heaven is supposed to be
i still rub the wolf's tooth around my neck
till i get them
to where they have to go

and after that
the rest is still not easy

It's Always 1923

it's warm out for january
40 degrees
warm at 40 and rain
still coming down from the night before but
dandy has to go out
so we head for the park
as we walk
it's warm

inside the park is another world
the fog is swirling
solomon is there with prince
the old man and his ragged dog
covered in haze both of them

only solomon is there
howling about everything
about governments
about 20th century music
prices classes of people religion
types of people
the nationalities of people
the products of government
the products of people
a real minor celine
but only because it's a minor park
as some kid called it
while trying to hack down
one of the elms with his baseball bat

given the proper setting
                    who knows

anyway it's all no good
the only thing good is opera
and polish anti-semitism
which made him leave
when the austrians left

It's Not just Another Sunday

we're both too tired to move
at 10 in the morning
after too much food
too much wine
and just enough love

it's gray outside

i touch your head
as you curl under my arm
and edith piaf
is hovering nearby
protecting us

i feel lucky
for the rest of the day
even though it's snowing
on the first of spring

The Piano Player

when i lived on ludlow street
when it was just ludlow street
and mostly quiet at night

in winter
            with a very light snow falling
from my window i'd
see charles aznavour his
collar always turned up against the cold
crossing that same narrow street in paris
with a light snow falling

Solitude

it's about thirty five degrees outside
up on top it's closer to thirty
and the air is perfect this late november
for using a hand saw to cut down
some of the smaller trees

it's quiet
except for a few crows
that live a little to the north
and a little to the east
of where i'm working

the sun is out
it's quiet and still
except for those crows
and the sound of one goose
flying overhead
into the southwest
forming its own v

Walking up Beeman Hill

walking up beeman hill in october
the road is broken and exposed
as a dried stream bed is
the moon is climbing and
thin clouds block just about half the stars
the clouds over the face of the moon
give the impression of gauze
over the face of a mummified prince
the dog and the boy cat
are climbing the hill with me

there's the intoxicating smell of wood smoke

looking south it's all cloud
where venus should be

at the top it's all quiet

there's an opening between the hemlocks
that looks to the top of the world
at this place
and out to the farm house just lit
whose name is the name of the road that leads to it

after a minute or two
the clouds north and south start to break
one shooting star flies across the big dipper
and venus appears
the way you did

the snow is still falling lightly
and like the wink from someone beautiful

venus disappears

it makes me tremble on this high spot
the way you still make me tremble
with no effort at all

About the Author

James Goldiner was born in Brooklyn, N.Y. and graduated from Franklin & Marshall College in 1961. During his college years and for a while afterwards he worked on merchant ships. He spent the next forty years working for the New York City Dept. of Social Services as reflected in some of his poems. This is the first time a collection of his poetry has been published. It covers work written over a period of forty five years.

* 9 7 8 0 6 1 5 5 1 4 1 4 7 *